IT'S TIME TO LEARN ABOUT ANTEATERS

It's Time to Learn about Anteaters

Walter the Educator

Silent King Books
A WhichHead Entertainment Imprint

Copyright © 2025 by Walter the Educator

All rights reserved. No part of this book may be reproduced in any manner whatsoever without written per- mission except in the case of brief quotations embodied in critical articles and reviews.

First Printing, 2024

Disclaimer

This book is a literary work; the story is not about specific persons, locations, situations, and/or circumstances unless mentioned in a historical context. Any resemblance to real persons, locations, situations, and/or circumstances is coincidental. This book is for entertainment and informational purposes only. The author and publisher offer this information without warranties expressed or implied. No matter the grounds, neither the author nor the publisher will be accountable for any losses, injuries, or other damages caused by the reader's use of this book. The use of this book acknowledges an understanding and acceptance of this disclaimer.

It's Time to Learn about Anteaters is a collectible early learning book by Walter the Educator suitable for all ages belonging to Walter the Educator's Time to Eat Book Series. Collect more books at WaltertheEducator.com

USE THE EXTRA SPACE TO TAKE NOTES AND DOCUMENT YOUR MEMORIES

ANTEATERS

Anteaters are special, long and lean,

It's Time to Learn about
Anteaters

With a tongue so quick and very keen.

They sniff and search both day and night,

For tiny ants, a tasty bite!

Their nose is long, but not to smell,

It helps them reach inside so well.

With sticky tongues that stretch so far,

They slurp up bugs, how smart they are!

No teeth at all, but that's just fine,

Their tongue moves fast, a hundred times!

They gobble ants and termites too,

A hungry anteater knows what to do!

They have big claws, so sharp and strong,

For digging mounds all day long.

They swipe and scoop, then take a taste,

Not a single crumb goes to waste!

It's Time to Learn about
Anteaters

Some are big, and some are small,

The giant's the biggest of them all!

The tamandua climbs trees with grace,

While silky anteaters hide in place.

Their fur is thick, it keeps them warm,

And shields them safe from bugs that swarm.

With colors brown, and black, and white,

They blend in well, out of sight!

They walk so funny, on their toes,

With claws curled up, so they don't poke holes.

Their stride is slow, but they don't mind,

They're built to sniff and dig and find!

Anteaters live where jungles grow,

Where rivers run and breezes blow.

In grasslands too, they roam around,

It's Time to Learn about
Anteaters

Where lots of crawling bugs are found!

Mothers carry babies tight,

Riding safely day and night.

On her back, the baby stays,

Learning all her anteater ways!

So now you know, so fun to meet,

An anteater with its snout so neat!

If you see one, say hello,

It's Time to Learn about
Anteaters

But let it eat and watch it go!

ABOUT THE CREATOR

Walter the Educator is one of the pseudonyms for Walter Anderson. Formally educated in Chemistry, Business, and Education, he is an educator, an author, a diverse entrepreneur, and he is the son of a disabled war veteran. "Walter the Educator" shares his time between educating and creating. He holds interests and owns several creative projects that entertain, enlighten, enhance, and educate, hoping to inspire and motivate you. Follow, find new works, and stay up to date with Walter the Educator™

at WaltertheEducator.com

www.ingramcontent.com/pod-product-compliance
Lightning Source LLC
LaVergne TN
LVHW052016060526
838201LV00059B/4062